THIS BOOK BELONGS TO

....

I Spy with My Little Eyes something Beginning with...

A

is for

Angel !

I Spy with My Little Eyes something Beginning with...

B

is for

Bauble !

I Spy with My Little Eyes something Beginning with...

C

C

is for

Candy cane !

I Spy with My Little Eyes something Beginning with...

D

is for

DECEMBER

25

December !

I Spy with My Little Eyes something Beginning with...

E

is for

Elf !

I Spy with My Little Eyes something Beginning with...

F

is for

Fireplace !

I Spy with My Little Eyes something Beginning with...

G

G

is for

Gingerbread!

I Spy with My Little Eyes
something Beginning with...

H

is for

Holly!

I Spy with My Little Eyes something Beginning with...

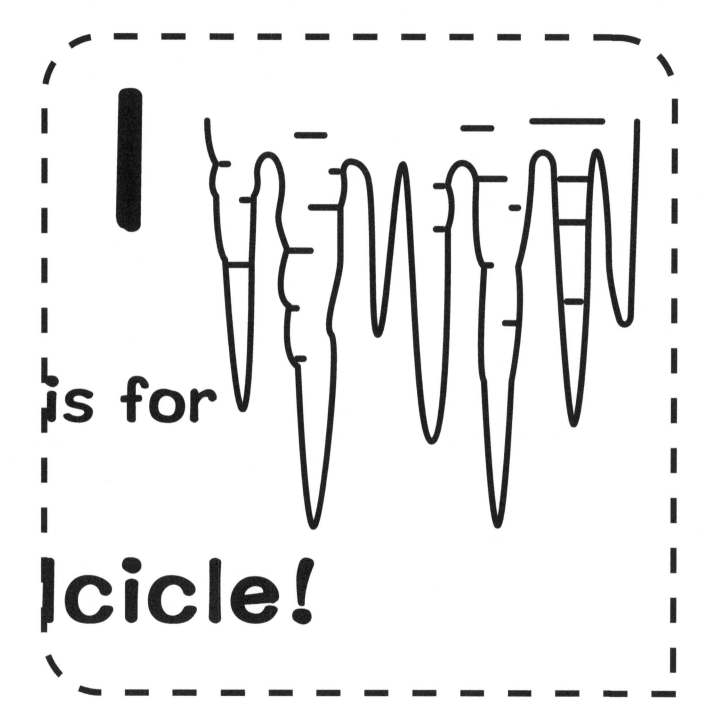

is for

Icicle!

I Spy with My Little Eyes something Beginning with...

J

is for

Jingle bells!

I Spy with My Little Eyes something Beginning with...

K

is for

Kindness !

L is for

to Santa

Letter to Santa!

M

is for

Mistletoe!

I Spy with My Little Eyes something Beginning with...

N

is for

North Pole!

I Spy with My Little Eyes something Beginning with...

O is for Ornament!

I Spy with My Little Eyes something Beginning with...

P

is for

Pine tree!

I Spy with My Little Eyes something Beginning with...

Q
is for
Quince!

R

is for

Reindeer!

I Spy with My Little Eyes
something Beginning with...

S

S

is for

Santa Claus!

I Spy with My Little Eyes something Beginning with...

T

is for

Turkey!

I Spy with My Little Eyes something Beginning with...

U

is for

Unwrap!

I Spy with My Little Eyes something Beginning with...

V

is for

Vacation!

I Spy with My Little Eyes something Beginning with...

W

is for

Wreath!

I Spy with My Little Eyes something Beginning with...

X is for Xmas!

I Spy with My Little Eyes something Beginning with...

Y

is for

Yule log!

I Spy with My Little Eyes something Beginning with...

Z
is for
Zeal!

Made in the USA
Las Vegas, NV
24 November 2023